THE ULTIMATE JOURNAL
For Long-Distance Couples
For Her

Dedication

To my partner and best friend, Charles, who reminds me every day that distance is just a measurement, and true closeness is found in the heart.

Thank you for being my constant inspiration, my mirror for growth, and the reason this book exists.

© 2025 ElevateWorks Publishing. All rights reserved. No part of this publication may be reproduced, distributed, or transmitted in any form or by any means, including photocopying, recording, or other electronic or mechanical methods, without the prior written permission of the author, except in the case of brief quotations embodied in critical reviews and certain other noncommercial uses permitted by copyright law.

How to use this book?

This journal is designed to strengthen the bond between partners who are temporarily or long-distance separated. Each day features a question and space for reflection—along with a quote that can spark further conversation. You and your partner can each fill out your own copy, or you can write each other's answers to deepen empathy and connection. Don't forget to discuss your responses over a call, text, or in person to learn more about one another, spark deeper connections, or simply share a laugh on the more lighthearted days.

- **Answer Flexibly**: If a specific question (e.g., "Which teacher had a lasting impression?") doesn't resonate, broaden the concept. Think of anyone who left a mark on you.

- **Weekly Reflection or Mini-Challenge**: Every 7th day, you'll find a prompt for deeper reflection or a fun challenge—use these as a chance to pause and recharge together.

- **Personal Touch**: Feel free to add doodles, stickers, or whatever best expresses your thoughts.

Above all, enjoy exploring each other's perspectives, celebrating your similarities, and cherishing your differences along the way!

A Look Inside Each Page

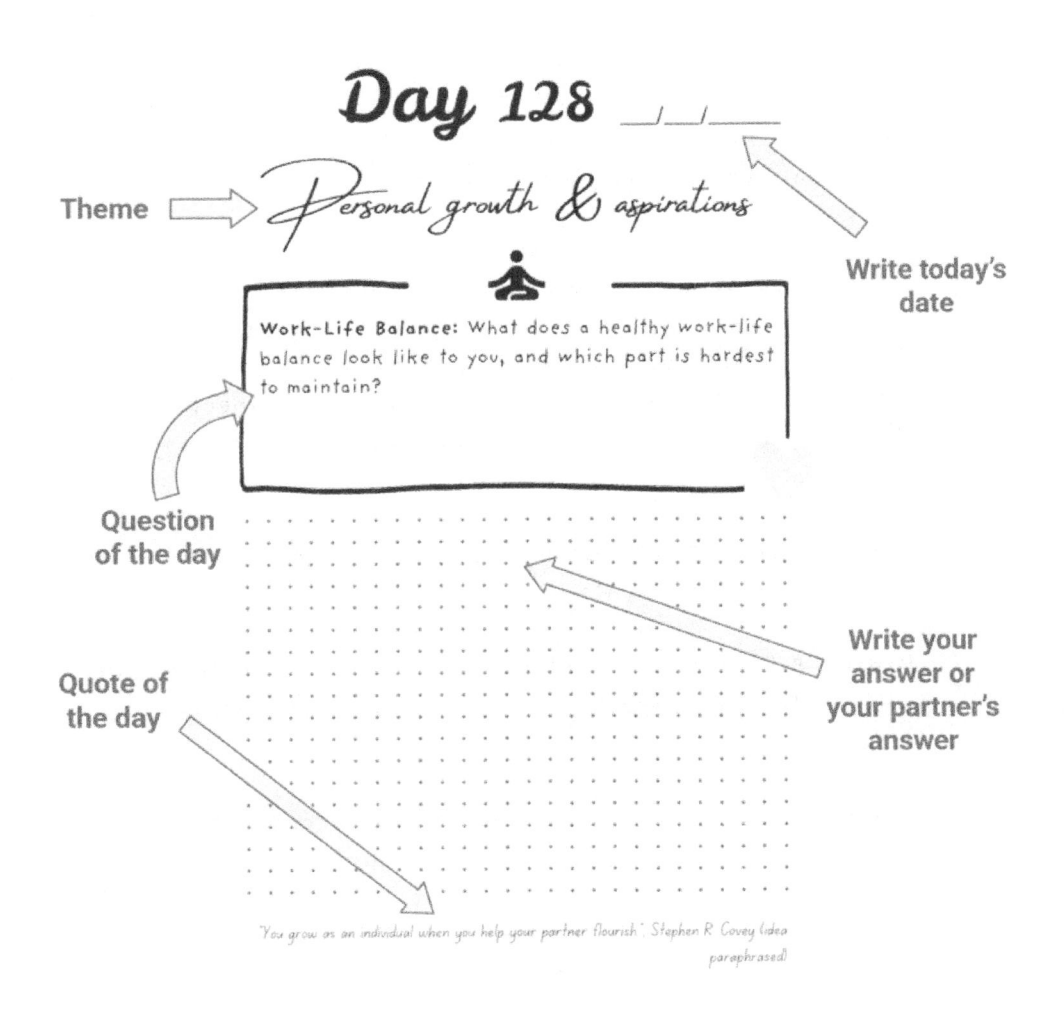

Day 128 __/__/__

Theme ➡ *Personal growth & aspirations*

Write today's date

Work-Life Balance: What does a healthy work-life balance look like to you, and which part is hardest to maintain?

Question of the day

Write your answer or your partner's answer

Quote of the day

"You grow as an individual when you help your partner flourish". Stephen R. Covey (idea paraphrased)

Themes overview

Below are the themes you'll find throughout the book. They appear in no particular order—just like real life, where surprises and deeper insights can pop up at any moment.

- **Learn More About Your Partner** — Uncover their perspectives, interests, and hidden quirks you might not have known.

- **Intimacy & Vulnerability** — Deepen emotional connections through open, heartfelt sharing about inner thoughts and feelings.

- **Communication & Conflict** — Strengthen listening skills, learn to resolve disagreements, and build healthier dialogue habits.

- **Dreams & Fantasies** — Explore each other's imaginative realms and playful 'what ifs' that spark inspiration (or just plain fun).

- **Daring** — Take small risks or push comfort zones, encouraging each other to try new things and grow together.

- **Funny Fun Facts** — Lighthearted questions to keep things playful, laugh together, and maintain that spark of curiosity.

- **Weekly Reflection** — A day to step back, review the previous week's discoveries, and gain clarity for the path ahead.

- **Childhood & Memories** — Reflect on formative experiences, revealing how the past shaped who you both are today.

- **Psychology** — Examine motives, behavior, and deeper mental processes, helping you understand yourselves and each other more fully.

- **Personal Growth & Aspirations** — Focus on individual goals and progress, supporting one another's ongoing evolution.

- **Mini-Challenge** — Fun or reflective tasks designed to break the routine, spark creative thinking, and bring you closer.

- **Shared Future & Goals** — Plan for the long term, discussing dreams and ambitions you can work toward as a team.

- **Shared Experiences** — Relive moments you've had together—or those you'd love to have soon—to celebrate your unique journey as a couple.

Why this book?

Long-distance or life's busy schedules can make it challenging to stay emotionally connected with your partner. This guided journal is designed to bridge that gap by offering daily prompts and reflections that spark deeper conversations, encouraging mutual understanding and closeness. My hope is that by dedicating just a few minutes each day to these questions and exercises, you'll discover new facets of each other, nurture a stronger bond, and keep the spark alive—no matter the physical distance.

Disclaimer: While this journal can help prompt meaningful conversations, it is not a substitute for professional psychological or relationship counseling. If you are experiencing ongoing emotional, mental health, or relationship difficulties, please seek guidance from a qualified professional.

About the Author

My name is Justine, and I've personally experienced the ups and downs of a long-distance relationship for five years before finally closing the gap with the love of my life. This book is born out of that journey—countless messages, midnight calls, and creative ways my husband and I stayed deeply connected despite the miles between us.

Over the years, we heard it all: "Long-distance never works," "It won't last," and other skepticism that could have shaken our resolve. Yet we proved them wrong. Now, I'm passionate about helping others do the same. Inside these pages, you'll find prompts and activities aimed at fostering the kind of meaningful, heart-to-heart bond that made our love story so strong. Because distance isn't an end—it's just another chapter in a relationship that can grow closer with every page you share.

Thank you

Thank you for purchasing this book and investing in the connection with your partner. Your support means so much to me. If you found value in these pages—or even if you have suggestions for improvement—I would appreciate an honest review on Amazon. Each review helps more people discover this resource and nurture stronger bonds in their own relationships

Placeholder for your photo

Attach or paste a photo of you and your partner here to remind you both of the strength and love you share.

Day 1   __/__/____

Intimacy & vulnerability

♡

Defining Intimacy: In your own words, how do you define "intimacy," and why is it important in a relationship?

"The meeting of two personalities is like the contact of two chemical substances: if there is any reaction, both are transformed." Carl Jung

Day 2 __/__/____

Learn more about your partner

Unexplored Talent: What's a talent you haven't had the chance to explore fully, and what would you like to do with it?

"Affection is responsible for nine-tenths of whatever solid and durable happiness there is in our natural lives.", C.S. Lewis

Day 3
___/___/____

Communication & conflict

Healthy Debates: Do you think disagreements can be productive? How do you turn a conflict into a constructive dialogue?

"Nothing is mysterious, no human relation. Except love.", Susan Sontag

Day 4 ___/___/___

Dreams and fantasies

Ultimate Superpower: If you could choose any superpower, but only use it for good, what would it be and why?

"Being heard is so close to being loved that for the average person, they are almost indistinguishable.", David Augsburger

Day 5   __/__/__

Daring

Impromptu Dance: Turn on your favorite song and have an impromptu dance party for one song.

"A good marriage is one which allows for change and growth in the individuals and in the way they express their love.", Pearl S. Buck

Day 6 __/__/____

Funny fun facts

Culinary Catastrophe: Describe your most epic cooking fail. What were you attempting to make?

"Communication leads to community, that is, to understanding, intimacy and mutual valuing.", Rollo May

Day 7   __/__/__

Weekly reflection

Highlight & Gratitude: What was the single best moment from this week, and why are you grateful for it?

"Intimacy requires courage because risk is inescapable.", Rollo May

Day 8   __/__/____

Childhood & memories

Favorite Game: Which childhood game brought you the most joy, and who did you usually play it with?

"We are born in relationship, we are wounded in relationship, and we can be healed in relationship.", Harville Hendrix

Day 9 __/__/__

Psychology

The Island Metaphor: Imagine you're stranded on a deserted island. What three objects would you have with you, and why? Discuss what these choices reveal about your priorities and survival instincts.[1]

---

[1] Objects chosen often represent priorities or survival instincts. For example, practical items suggest pragmatism, while sentimental items indicate value in memories or relationships.

Day 10 __/__/____

Intimacy & vulnerability

♡

Trust Foundation: What does "trust" specifically look and feel like to you, and how can your partner help maintain that trust?

"The heart has its reasons, which reason knows nothing of.", Blaise Pascal

Day 11 ___/___/___

Personal growth & aspirations

Personal Mission Statement: If you had to write a one-sentence mission statement for your life, what would it be?

"Compassion is a verb.", Thich Nhat Hanh

Day 12 __/__/____

Funny fun facts

😄

Unintentional Comedy: What's something you did that was meant to be serious but ended up being hilariously funny?

"In a full heart there is room for everything, and in an empty heart there is room for nothing.", Antonio Porchia

Day 13 __/__/__

Learn more about your partner

Life's Soundtrack: If you could pick three songs to represent different phases of your life so far, which songs would you choose and why?

"The heart that breaks open can contain the whole universe.", Joanna Macy

Day 14 __/__/____

Mini-challenge

✓

Nonsensical Riddle: Invent a bizarre riddle or joke (e.g., "Why did the cucumber join the circus?") and have your partner guess the punchline. It doesn't have to make sense—absurd answers encouraged!

"A great relationship is about two things: first, appreciating the similarities, and second, respecting the differences.", Unknown

Day 15   __/__/____

Intimacy & vulnerability

♡

Emotional Safety: When do you feel most emotionally safe to be fully yourself around your partner?

"The highest form of knowledge is empathy.", Bill Bullard

Day 16 __/__/____

Childhood & memories

Childhood Fears: What was your biggest childhood fear, and how did you eventually overcome it?

"The bond that links your true family is not one of blood, but of respect and joy in each other's life.", Richard Bach

Day 17   __/__/__

Shared future & goals

Big Picture Dream: When you imagine our future together, what's the first image or scenario that comes to mind?

"A kiss is a secret told to the mouth instead of the ear.", Ingrid Bergman

Day 18 __/__/__

Shared experiences

Virtual Travel Night: Choose a country you both dream of visiting. Spend the evening exploring its culture online together, from virtual museum tours to travel videos, and plan your dream visit.

"To give and then not feel that one has given is the very best of all ways of giving.",
Max Beerbohm

Day 19   __/__/__

Daring

⚡

Accent Imitation: Speak in an accent chosen by your partner for the next 5 minutes of the conversation.

"It is not how much we give, but how much we put into giving.", Mother Teresa

Day 20 __/__/____

Psychology

Animal Spirit: If you could be any animal, which one would you be and why? Discuss what this choice says about your personality and aspirations.[1]

---

[1] The chosen animal can reflect how your partner sees themselves or aspires to be. Predators might signify leadership and strength, while social animals suggest the importance of community.

Day 21 __/__/__

Weekly reflection

> **Partner Insight:** What's one new insight you gained about your partner or their perspective this week?

"To handle yourself, use your head; to handle others, use your heart.", Eleanor Roosevelt

Day 22 __/__/____

Personal growth & aspirations

Greatest Fear: What personal fear are you determined to overcome, and why is it important to you?

"Friendship is essentially a partnership.", Aristotle

Day 23   __/__/__

Dreams and fantasies

Time Machine Travel: If we had a time machine for one day, which era would you want us to visit together, and what would we do?

"True kindness presupposes the faculty of imagining as one's own the suffering and joy of others.", Andre Gide

Day 24 __/__/__

Learn more about your partner

Dream Project: What's a dream project you'd love to work on, and what makes it exciting to you?

"Embrace the glorious mess that you are.", Elizabeth Gilbert

Day 25 __/__/__

Shared future & goals

Home Sweet Home: What does your dream living situation look like—city loft, countryside cottage, mobile tiny home, etc.?

"Our wounds are often the openings into the best and most beautiful part of us.", David Richo

Day 26 __/__/____

Personal growth & aspirations

Defining Success: How do you personally define success, and in what ways have you reached or are you reaching your definition of it?

"A heart without dreams is like a bird without feathers.", Suzy Kassem

Day 27 __/__/__

Funny fun facts

😄

DIY Gone Wrong: What's a DIY project you attempted that turned out nothing like you planned?

"Intimacy is the capacity to be rather weird with someone—and finding that that's okay with them.", Alain de Botton

Day 28 __/__/____

Mini-challenge

✓

> **Gratitude Photo Exchange:** Each of you snaps a photo of something you're grateful for in your day and shares it.

"When hearts align, even whispered wishes echo like thunder.", Edna St. Vincent Millay (poetic paraphrase)

Day 29   __/__/__

Communication & conflict

> **Tone of Voice:** How does someone's tone of voice affect your response in a heated discussion?

"No road is long with good company.", Turkish Proverb

Day 30 __/__/____

Learn more about your partner

Fictional World: If you could live in any fictional world for a year, where would it be and what would you do there?

"A single rose can be my garden... a single friend, my world.", Leo Buscaglia

Day 31 __/__/__

Psychology

Dream Job as a Child: What was your dream job as a child, and how has your perspective on this dream changed over time?[1]

---

[1] Changes in dream jobs can reflect personal growth, shifting values, or practical adaptations to life's realities. It's a window into your partner's evolution over time.

Day 32 ___/___/___

Personal growth & aspirations

> **Self-Care Rituals:** What rituals or habits do you practice for self-care, and how do they help you stay balanced?

"Soul meets soul on the lips of lovers.", Percy Bysshe Shelley

Day 33 ___/___/___

Childhood & memories

Childhood Mentor: Other than a parent, was there an adult in your life who had a lasting positive impact on you?

"Affection is never wasted. If it is not reciprocated, it flows back and softens the heart.", Washington Irving

Day 34 __/__/__

Communication & conflict

Listening Style: When your partner talks, do you tend to listen to understand or listen to respond? How can you improve?

"The only way to have a friend is to be one.", Ralph Waldo Emerson

Day 35 ___/___/___

Weekly reflection

Emotional Check-In: Which emotion surfaced most often over the past six days, and what triggered it?

"Shared joy is a double joy; shared sorrow is half a sorrow.", Swedish Proverb

Day 36   __/__/____

Fun & romance

Date Bucket List: If we could plan three dream dates right now (with no constraints on time or money), what would they be?

"Tenderness and kindness are not signs of weakness and despair, but manifestations of strength and resolution.", Kahlil Gibran

Day 37 __/__/__

Dreams and fantasies

Fantasy Pet: Imagine if you could have any creature, real or mythical, as a pet. What would it be and what name would you give it?

"The most precious gift we can offer others is our presence.", Thich Nhat Hanh

Day 38 __/__/__

Shared future & goals

Career Aspirations: How do you see our individual career goals fitting together, and what support do you need along the way?

"The pain of parting is nothing to the joy of meeting again.", Charles Dickens

Day 39 ___/___/___

Communication & conflict

Text vs. Talk: Do you prefer handling sensitive topics via text or face-to-face? Why do you think that is?

"He who cannot forgive destroys the bridge over which he himself must pass.", George Herbert

Day 40 __/__/__

Psychology

The Mirror Exercise: Stand in front of a mirror for two minutes, then write down all the thoughts that went through your mind. Discuss how self-perception affects your confidence and daily life.[1]

---

[1] Thoughts during this exercise can reveal self-esteem levels and self-perception. Positive thoughts suggest confidence, while critical thoughts might indicate areas of insecurity.

Day 41 __/__/____

Funny fun facts

Sudden Spotlight: Have you ever found yourself unexpectedly the center of attention for something silly or embarrassing? What was the situation?

"Blessed are the hearts that can bend; they shall never be broken.", Albert Camus

Day 42 __/__/____

Mini-challenge

✓

Recipe Swap: Exchange a simple recipe and cook it "together" via video chat, then taste-test simultaneously.

"Let us be grateful to people who make us happy, they are the charming gardeners who make our souls blossom.", Marcel Proust

Day 43   __/__/____

Childhood & memories

Embarrassing School Moment: What's one funny or embarrassing moment from school that you still remember vividly?

"Happiness is only real when shared.", Christopher McCandless

Day 44 __/__/____

Learn more about your partner

Signature Dish: If you had to cook one dish that best represents you, what would it be and what's the story behind it?

"In the sweetness of friendship let there be laughter, and sharing of pleasures.", Kahlil Gibran

Day 45 __/__/__

Fun & romance

> **Spontaneous Adventures:** What's something spontaneous you've always wanted to do with me but haven't yet?

"Whoever is happy will make others happy too.", Anne Frank

Day 46 __/__/__

Dreams and fantasies

Perfect World: What would your version of a perfect world include? How would it differ from the world we live in now?

"We do not see things as they are, we see them as we are.", Anais Nin

Day 47 __/__/____

Funny fun facts

Public Speaking Blunders: Have you ever said something completely wrong or funny during a public speaking moment?

"A gentle heart is tied with an easy thread.", George Herbert

Day 48 __/__/____

Shared future & goals

Financial Philosophy: What's your approach to saving, spending, and investing for the long term, and how can we align on it?

"To be kind is more important than to be right. Many people need a patient heart that listens.", Unknown

Day 49 __/__/__

Weekly reflection

Self-Care Check: How well did you take care of your physical and emotional needs this week?

"Feelings are much like waves; we can't stop them, but we can choose which ones to surf.", Jonatan Martensson

Day 50 __/__/____

Daring

⚡

Blind Drawing: Blindfold yourself and attempt to draw a portrait of your partner, then reveal the results.

"One sees clearly only with the heart. Anything essential is invisible to the eyes.", Antoine de Saint-Exupery

Day 51 ___/___/___

Dreams and fantasies

Ultimate Feast: If you could have any dish from anywhere in the world right now, what would it be and why?

"When we quit thinking primarily about ourselves, we undergo a heroic transformation of consciousness.", Joseph Campbell

Day 52 ___/___/___

Personal growth & aspirations

Growth vs. Comfort: When faced with a choice between staying in your comfort zone or challenging yourself, how do you decide?

"Deep connection is the root of true understanding.", Unknown

Day 53 __/__/__

Shared future & goals

Family Vision: If you imagine having children (or not), how do you see that playing out in our relationship's future?

"Real closeness is the result of shared vulnerability.", Unknown

Day 54 __/__/____

Fun & romance

Silliest Moment: What's the funniest moment we've shared that always makes you laugh when you think about it?

"Romance is the gentle spark that ignites hearts without burning them.", Unknown

Day 55 ___/___/___

Funny fun facts

Gift Mishaps: What's the funniest or most inappropriate gift you've ever received?

"Connection is why we're here; it is what gives purpose and meaning to our lives.", Brene Brown

Day 56 __/__/____

Mini-challenge

✓

One-Hour Off-Grid: Both agree to disconnect from devices (except for an emergency line) for an hour and do something restorative. Share what you did afterwards.

"True friendship comes when the silence between two people is comfortable.", David Tyson

Day 57   __/__/__

Shared experiences

Online Game Marathon: Pick several free online games you can play together. Include a mix of strategy, adventure, and casual games for a fun-filled night.

"A healthy relationship is one where you can be your true self without fear.", Unknown

Day 58 __/__/____

Learn more about your partner

Heroic Moment: Can you recall a time when you did something you considered truly brave? What motivated you?

"Trust is the glue of life. It's the foundational principle that holds all relationships.",
Stephen R. Covey

Day 59 ___/___/___

Intimacy & vulnerability

♡

Being Seen: What's something you've never told anyone because you worry they might judge you?

"Distance means so little when someone means so much.", Tom McNeal (Shortened paraphrase)

Day 60 __/__/____

Funny fun facts

Name Mix-ups: Have you ever called someone by the wrong name at the worst possible time? Who was it?

"In the end there doesn't have to be anyone who understands you. There just has to be someone who wants to.", Robert Brault

Day 61   __/__/__

Personal growth & aspirations

Skills to Learn: Which new skill or hobby would you love to master in the next year?

"The strength of a relationship lies in honor, not in power.", Morgan Scott Peck (M. Scott Peck, paraphrased)

Day 62 ___/___/___

Childhood & memories

First Best Friend: Who was your first best friend, and what made your friendship special?

"The most important thing in communication is hearing what isn't said.", Peter F. Drucker

Day 63   __/__/____

Weekly reflection

Moments of Joy: Identify a small, seemingly insignificant moment that made you unexpectedly happy this week.

"A great relationship is about two things: appreciating each other and growing together.", Unknown

Day 64 __/__/____

Dreams and fantasies

Secret Hideaway: Describe your ideal secret hideaway. Where would it be, and what would it look like?

"No matter how far you go, a good heart will bring you near.", African Proverb

Day 65 __/__/__

Fun & romance

> **Nicknames & Inside Jokes:** Do we have a favorite inside joke or nickname that never fails to make you smile?

"True enchantment appears when you dare to be playful in each other's presence.",
Unknown

Day 66 __/__/____

Shared experiences

DIY Craft Challenge: Choose a simple craft or DIY project to do together over video call. Compare your creations and maybe even mail them to each other as keepsakes.

"Intimacy grows in the soil of vulnerability.", John Gottman (idea paraphrased)

Day 67 ___/___/___

Personal growth & aspirations

Core Values: What are your top three core values, and how do they guide your everyday decisions?

"Love may be blind, but empathy sees everything.", Unknown

Day 68 __/__/____

Learn more about your partner

Forgotten Hobby: Is there a hobby you loved as a child but stopped doing? Would you ever consider picking it up again?

"A strong relationship requires choosing to love each other even in those moments when you struggle to like each other.", Unknown

Day 69 __/__/__

Fun & romance

Playful Teasing: Is there a playful tease or banter we have that you secretly love?

"You know you're in love when you can't sleep because reality is better than your dreams.", Dr. Seuss

Day 70 __/__/____

Mini-challenge

✓

Kindness Challenge: Each do one random act of kindness for a stranger or friend, then report back how it felt.

"He who loves 50 people has 50 woes; he who loves no one has no woes.", Buddha (Traditional attribution)

Day 71 ___/___/___

Childhood & memories

Extended Family: Describe one relative (e.g., grandparent, aunt, uncle) who significantly influenced your childhood.

"Without respect, no lasting connection can exist.", Unknown

Day 72 __/__/__

Communication & conflict

Trigger Words: Are there certain words or phrases that instantly put you on the defensive?

"Storms make trees take deeper roots.", Dolly Parton (Metaphor often applied to relationships)

Day 73 __/__/__

Psychology

The Three Fears: Share three things you're afraid of and discuss why. Explore how these fears impact your decisions and behavior.[1]

---

[1] Common fears often relate to loss, failure, or rejection. Understanding these can help you comprehend your partner's protective behaviors or hesitations.

Day 74 __/__/____

Funny fun facts

Awkward Autocorrect: Share your most embarrassing autocorrect fail in a text or email.

"Maturity is learning to love some people and still step away from them.", Unknown

Day 75 ___/___/___

Intimacy & vulnerability

Showing Affection: How do you prefer to show physical or emotional affection? Do you think it matches how your partner prefers to receive it?

"Believing the best in one another is the foundation of unshakable closeness.", Unknown

Day 76 ___/___/___

Learn more about your partner

Cultural Tradition: What's a cultural tradition you love? How does it connect you to your roots?

"Friendship doubles your joys and divides your sorrows.", Unknown (common proverb)

Day 77 __/__/__

Weekly reflection

Intimacy Boost: Did you feel more connected or distant with your partner this week? Why?

"A good relationship is when two people accept each other's past, support each other's present, and encourage each other's future.", Unknown

Day 78   __/__/__

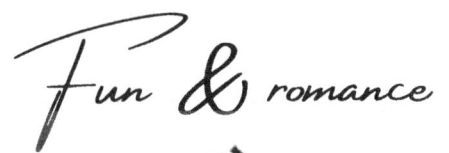

Fun & romance

Dance With Me: Do you enjoy slow dancing or dancing in general? If so, what song would you love to slow dance to together?

"A long-distance bond is a test of how far affection can travel.", Unknown

Day 79 __/__/__

Funny fun facts

😄

Surprise Party Spoiler: Have you ever spoiled a surprise party or been the one whose surprise was spoiled?

"Emotional availability is more precious than any gift you can give.", Unknown

Day 80   __/__/____

Shared experiences

Star Gazing: If you both have access to a clear sky, spend some time stargazing while on call. Use an app to help identify stars and constellations you both can see.

"A single conversation across the table with a wise person is worth a month's study of books.", Chinese Proverb

Day 81 __/__/__

Daring

⚡

Reveal Your Screen: Share your phone or computer screen for a minute, letting your partner see what tabs or apps you have open.

"Healthy relationships are built on boundaries, not on blurred lines.", Unknown

Day 82 __/__/__

Childhood & memories

Nicknames: Did you have any nicknames growing up, and what's the story behind them?

"No relationship is all sunshine, but two people can share one umbrella and survive the storm together.", Unknown

Day 83 ___/___/___

Personal growth & aspirations

Overcoming Self-Doubt: Can you recall a time you struggled with self-doubt, and what helped you push through?

"Listening is an act of love.", David Isay (Founder of StoryCorps)

Day 84 ___/___/___

Mini-challenge

✓

Sticky-Note Love: Write a short love note or encouragement message and stick it somewhere unexpected

"Love is not about property, diamonds, and gifts. It is about sharing your very self with the world around you.", Pope Francis (Short paraphrase)

Day 85   __/__/__

Communication & conflict

> **Explaining Emotions:** Do you find it challenging to articulate your emotions during conflict? What helps you express them more clearly?

"Affection is not measured by distance but by depth.", Tagalog Proverb (paraphrased)

Day 86 __/__/__

Daring

Imaginary Friend Introduction: Introduce your partner to an imaginary friend, giving them a detailed backstory and personality.

"In a relationship, each person should support the other; they lift each other up.", Taylor Swift (Short paraphrase)

Day 87 ___/___/___

Shared experiences

Virtual Picnic: Set up a picnic vibe in your own spaces and share a meal over video call. You can even try to synchronize your meals to match each other's.

"To go fast, go alone. To go far, go together.", African Proverb

Day 88 __/__/____

Personal growth & aspirations

Vision Board: If you created a vision board for your future, what key images or words would definitely be on it?

"The universe only makes sense when we have someone to share our feelings with.",
Paulo Coelho (Short paraphrase)

Day 89 __/__/__

Fun & romance

> **Childlike Fun:** What's a kid-like activity (e.g., building a fort, finger-painting) you'd love us to do just for fun?

"Absence sharpens affection, while presence strengthens commitment.", Unknown

Day 90   __/__/____

Daring

Cold Shower Reaction: Take the phone into the bathroom, turn the shower to cold, and record your reaction to the cold water (Be careful!)

"What you do speaks so loudly that I cannot hear what you say.", Ralph Waldo Emerson

Day 91 ___/___/___

Weekly reflection

Personal Achievement: What personal achievement —no matter how tiny—are you proudest of since last reflection?

"Growth is painful. Change is painful. But nothing is as painful as staying somewhere you don't belong.", Mandy Hale

Day 92 __/__/____

Learn more about your partner

Unexpected Book: What book has influenced you in a way you didn't expect? How did it change your perspective?

"Every happy couple has learned how to care more about the relationship than winning arguments.", Unknown

Day 93 ___/___/___

Childhood & memories

Family Home: Think of your childhood home. What specific room or spot holds the most memories for you?

"Security is not owning a person, but trusting them.", Unknown

Day 94   __/__/__

Funny fun facts

Travel Tribulations: What's a funny travel story or mishap you've experienced?

"If you want a deep connection, show your heart; that's what hearts are for.", Terry Real (Relationship therapist, paraphrased)

Day 95 ___/___/___

Psychology

Happiness Ingredients: List five things that make you genuinely happy and discuss how you can incorporate more of these into your daily life.[1]

---

[1] These elements highlight what your partner values most for personal fulfillment. Recurring themes can indicate areas where they seek support or shared experiences.

Day 96

___/___/____

Shared future & goals

Location Preferences: Do you see yourself living in multiple places over time, or putting down roots in one spot?

"Sometimes we see our reflection in someone else's eyes better than in our own mirror.",
Unknown

Day 97   __/__/__

Daring

⚡

> **Celebrity Impersonation:** Do your best impersonation of a celebrity chosen by your partner.

"True closeness is when you can show your scars and still feel safe.", Unknown

Day 98 ___/___/___

Mini-challenge

Create a Joint Playlist: Each partner adds 5 songs to a shared playlist that captures your mood or relationship vibe.

"Great couples are simply two people who refuse to give up on each other.", Unknown

Day 99 __/__/____

Personal growth & aspirations

Time-Travel Advice: If you could go back five years and give yourself advice, what would you say?

"You can't force chemistry to exist, but you can nurture it when it does.", Unknown

Day 100 __/__/__

Shared experiences

Home Movie Festival: Share childhood videos or your favorite movie clips with each other. It's a great way to learn more about your partner's past and preferences.

"Cultivate the ground you stand on together, and both of you will grow.", Unknown

Day 101 ___/___/___

Funny fun facts

☺

School Project Gone Awry: Ever had a school project or presentation that didn't go as planned?

"Marriage is a mosaic you build with your spouse—millions of tiny moments create your love story.", Jennifer Smith (Short paraphrase)

Day 102 __/__/____

Shared future & goals

Lifestyle Pace: Do you envision a fast-paced city life, a slower rural pace, or a mix of both in different stages of our life?

"The person meant for you encourages you to be your best and sees your worst but still stays.", Unknown

Day 103 __/__/__

Fun & romance

Surprise Factor: What's the best surprise (big or small) you've ever planned for someone, and would you do it for me?

"A strong bond can handle truth, no matter how difficult.", Henry Cloud (Psychologist, paraphrased)

Day 104 __/__/____

Communication & conflict

> **Conflict Frequency:** How often do you think it's normal for couples to argue, and what does that say about a relationship?

"No relationship can survive without forgiveness. The one that fails to forgive breaks the bridge for themselves.", George Herbert (Paraphrased concept)

Day 105 __/__/__

Weekly reflection

Conflict Analysis: Think of a minor conflict or disagreement that arose. What would you do the same or differently next time?

"Distance is just a test of how true a connection can be.", Unknown

Day 106 __/__/____

Shared experiences

Fitness Challenge: Choose a workout video online and do the workout together during a video call. It's a fun way to stay healthy and motivate each other.

"Real connection is not found in perfection, but in vulnerability.", Unknown

Day 107 ___/___/___

Learn more about your partner

Alternate Life: If you had chosen a completely different path in life, what would it have been and why?

"To know another fully is to discover the doors you never knew you had.", Carl Rogers (paraphrased)

Day 108 __/__/__

Daring

Yoga Pose Challenge: Attempt a challenging yoga pose and hold it for 30 seconds.

"Life shrinks or expands in proportion to one's courage—together, it expands even more.", Anais Nin (adapted)

Day 109 __/__/__

Communication & conflict

Personal Responsibility: How do you own your part in a conflict, and what's the hardest part about admitting fault?

"In conflict, we often defend the self we fear losing rather than meet the other with curiosity.", Marshall Rosenberg (concept)

Day 110 __/__/__

Fun & romance 🎉

> **Love in Pop Culture:** Is there a love song, movie, or book that you feel captures our relationship vibe?

"Romance is the glitter that makes everyday moments sparkle.", Nora Roberts (concept paraphrased)

Day 111 ___/___/___

Learn more about your partner

Unwinding Method: How do you prefer to unwind after a stressful period? What makes this method effective for you?

"Curiosity about each other keeps the heart awake.", John Gottman (idea paraphrased)

Day 112 __/__/__

Mini-challenge ✓

Show & Tell: Pick one meaningful object from your home and explain its backstory on a video call.

"A spirit of play in a relationship keeps it forever young.", Robert Fulghum (idea paraphrased)

Day 113 ___/___/___

Shared future & goals

Personal vs. Couple Goals: How do we balance our personal ambitions with our shared relationship goals?

"A common vision cements two hearts in a single purpose.", Stephen R. Covey (concept paraphrased)

Day 114 __/__/____

Intimacy & vulnerability

♡

Healing Together: How can partners help each other heal from past emotional wounds and insecurities?

"Intimacy begins the moment we learn to let go of our armor.", Robert Bly (idea paraphrased)

Day 115 ___/___/___

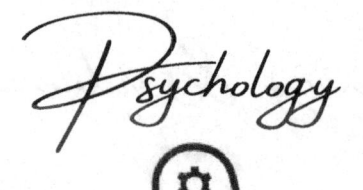

Psychology

Stress Triggers: Identify three major stress triggers in your life. Discuss coping strategies and how your partner can support you during stressful times.[1]

---

[1] Identifying stress triggers can help you understand your partner's reactions to certain situations and how you can offer support or alleviate stress.

Day 116 __/__/__

Childhood & memories

Dream Job as a Child: What was your dream job as a child, and how has your perspective on this dream changed over time?

"Shared childhood stories reveal the soil that shaped us.", Fred Rogers (concept paraphrased)

Day 117 __/__/__

Communication & conflict

> **Stonewalling:** Have you ever used silence or withdrawal as a tactic in arguments? How does it affect the outcome?

"Arguing can be the door to clarity if both hearts remain open.", M. Scott Peck (idea paraphrased)

Day 118   __/__/__

Funny fun facts

Wrong Place, Wrong Time: Ever walked into the wrong room or building and only realized it much later? What happened?

"Big egos are like heavy backpacks: tough to carry around in a relationship.", Elayne Boosler (comedian, paraphrased)

Day 119 __/__/__

Weekly reflection

Looking Ahead: What's one intention or goal you'd like to set for the upcoming week?

"The supreme happiness of life is the conviction that we are loved.", Victor Hugo

Day 120 __/__/__

Fun & romance

Favorite Physical Affection: What small physical gesture (like a forehead kiss, playful nudge) do you find the most endearing?

"A shared sense of humor is like a secret code for two souls.", Margaret Atwood (idea paraphrased)

Day 121 __/__/__

Childhood & memories

Family Moves: If you moved homes or changed schools as a child, how did it affect you and your friendships?

"Each memory recounted is a bridge between past innocence and present trust.", Maya Angelou (idea paraphrased)

Day 122 __/__/__

Dreams and fantasies

Fictional Job: If you could have any job in a fictional world, what would it be and in which universe?

"A shared dream is a potent force for uniting two minds.", Napoleon Hill (idea paraphrased)

Day 123 __/__/__

Shared experiences

Playlist Exchange: Create music playlists for each other and listen to them together during the call, discussing why you chose each song.

"Real bonding happens in the stories two people create together.", Donald Miller (concept paraphrased)

Day 124 __/__/__

Psychology

Life Soundtrack: Choose five songs that you feel represent different stages of your life. Share these with your partner and explain the significance of each.[1]

---

[1] The songs and their associated stages can reveal emotional highs and lows, significant life changes, or core memories that have shaped your partner's identity.

Day 125 __/__/__

Shared future & goals

Future Traditions: Are there any traditions you'd love us to establish (e.g., annual trips, holiday rituals) once we're more settled?

"Looking forward together is the surest way to keep the present vibrant.", John Maxwell (idea paraphrased)

Day 126 __/__/__

Weekly reflection

Step Out of Comfort: Did you try anything new or step outside your comfort zone this week? Describe the experience.

"When two souls share the same path, each step forward is done hand in hand.", George Eliot (inspired paraphrase)

Day 127 __/__/__

Funny fun facts

Outfit Oops: Have you ever left the house wearing clothes inside out or mismatched shoes without noticing? When did you find out?

"The trouble with some women is they get all excited about nothing—and then marry him.", Cher (humorous quip)

Day 128 __/__/____

Personal growth & aspirations

Work-Life Balance: What does a healthy work-life balance look like to you, and which part is hardest to maintain?

"You grow as an individual when you help your partner flourish.", Stephen R. Covey (idea paraphrased)

Day 129 ___/___/___

Shared experiences

Dream House Planning: Use generative AI tools to design or plan your dream house together. Discuss what each of you would like and why.

"Shared laughter is the shortest distance between two hearts.", Victor Borge (adapted)

Day 130 __/__/____

Communication & conflict

Finding the Right Moment: Do you think timing plays a big role in communication success? Why or why not?

"Speak to be heard; listen to be changed.", Stephen R. Covey (paraphrased)

Day 131 __/__/__

Childhood & memories

Childhood Adversities: Recall a challenging time in your childhood. What got you through it?

"Sometimes, to understand the adult before you, you must meet the child within them.",
Alice Miller (paraphrased)

Day 132 __/__/__

Daring

⚡

Improvised Song: Make up a song about your day and perform it.

"Be brave enough to break your own rules for the one who matters most.", Elif Shafak (paraphrased concept)

Day 133 __/__/__

Mini-challenge

✓

> **Try a New Skill:** Each pick one small "micro-skill" to learn (like folding origami, or a new workout move). Demonstrate to each other.

"Love is not a word here, but a shared act of faith in each other's unfolding beauty.",
Rainer Maria Rilke (adapted concept)

Day 134 __/__/____

Funny fun facts

Gadget Gaffes: What's the funniest or most embarrassing thing you've done because you didn't know how to use a gadget or appliance?

"Marriage is the only war in which you sleep with the enemy.", Francois de La Rochefoucauld (often attributed)

Day 135 __/__/__

Intimacy & vulnerability

♡

Emotional Discomfort: When someone gets too close emotionally, do you ever feel the urge to pull away? Why or why not?

"Vulnerability is the birthplace of genuine connection.", Brene Brown

Day 136 __/__/__

Personal growth & aspirations

Daily Habit: What is one daily habit you believe has the biggest impact on your growth?

"Two souls committed to growth spark each other's transformation.", Pierre Teilhard de Chardin (concept)

Day 137 __/__/__

Psychology

The Ultimate Day: Describe your idea of a perfect day from start to finish. What activities does it include, and who are you with?[1]

---

[1] This reflects your partner's idea of happiness and satisfaction. Look for elements of solitude vs. social interaction, adventure vs. relaxation, and creativity vs. consumption.

Day 138 __/__/____

Communication & conflict

> **Unspoken Tension:** How do you sense tension in the air before a conflict actually erupts, and what do you do about it?

"Friction can polish or wound; it's the choice of whether we attack or understand.", Dan Wile (couples therapist, concept paraphrased)

Day 139 __/__/__

Learn more about your partner

> **Inspiring Artwork:** Is there a piece of art (painting, sculpture, music, etc.) that deeply moves you? Describe its impact.

"Genuine interest in a person reveals them more than years of polite conversation.",
Robert Johnson (Jungian analyst, paraphrased)

Day 140 ___/___/___

Weekly reflection

Time Management: How balanced was your week in terms of work, rest, and fun? Any plans to adjust next week?

"The greatest relationships are built on a willingness to evolve side by side.", Wayne Dyer (concept paraphrased)

Day 141 ___/___/___

Shared future & goals

Retirement Daydream: If we were both retired (or financially free), how would you imagine spending an average day together?

"Couples who plan together stand firm in the winds of change.", Denis Waitley (concept paraphrased)

Day 142 __/__/____

Dreams and fantasies

Dream Invention: What's one invention that doesn't exist but would change your life for the better?

"Fantasy binds two people if they dare to explore the realm of possibility together.",
Anais Nin

Day 143 ___/___/___

Communication & conflict

Conflict Resolution Strategy: What's one conflict resolution strategy you've learned or developed that you find effective?

"Conflict is inevitable, but combat is optional.", Max Lucado

Day 144 ___/___/___

Shared experiences

Poetry or Short Story Night: Write poems or short stories for each other and then read them aloud during your call.

"Travel is sweeter when you carry each other's wonder.", Pico Iyer (concept paraphrased)

Day 145 __/__/__

Childhood & memories

Childhood Hero: As a kid, who did you look up to as a hero (real or fictional), and why?

"Embrace each other's younger selves; they hold the keys to hidden fears and joys.",
Clarissa Pinkola Estes (idea paraphrased)

Day 146 __/__/__

Personal growth & aspirations

Risk-Taking: Describe a risk you took that paid off. What motivated you to go for it?

"A relationship is the gym of the spirit, where each repetition makes you stronger.",
Robin Sharma (inspired paraphrase)

Day 147 __/__/__

Mini-challenge

✓

Vision Board Pic: Create a digital "vision board" snippet (like a collage) of your hopes or goals for the month. Compare boards.

"The best proof of commitment is loyalty that stands firm under stress.", Walter Anderson (Shortened)

Day 148 __/__/__

Shared experiences

Magic Moment: Learn magic tricks separately and perform them for each other during your video call.

"Two souls weaving memories become stronger in spirit.", Unknown proverb (often attributed)

Day 149 __/__/__

Communication & conflict

> **Intent vs. Impact:** Can you recall a time when your intention didn't match the impact your words had on your partner?

"Miscommunication is the root of many problems; mindful listening is its remedy.",
Henepola Gunaratana (concept paraphrased)

Day 150 __/__/__

Daring

Eat Something Spicy: Eat a spoonful of the spiciest thing you have in your kitchen.

"Courage in love means risking pride for truth.", Erich Fromm (idea paraphrased)

Day 151   __/__/__

Childhood & memories

Weird Habit: What is one quirky or weird habit you had as a child that makes you smile now?

"Our earliest impressions shape us; sharing them invites deeper compassion.", Bruno Bettelheim (concept)

Day 152 __/__/____

Psychology

The Gift of Time: If you had an extra hour every day, how would you spend it? Discuss how time management and priorities influence your relationship.[1]

---

[1] How your partner chooses to spend an extra hour can indicate what they feel is missing in their daily routine, whether it's relaxation, personal hobbies, or time with loved ones.

Day 153 __/__/__

Shared experiences

Fashion Show: Have a mini fashion show over a video call where you try on different outfits and get the other's opinion.

"People bond most when they brave life's storms side by side.", Helen Keller (idea paraphrased)

Day 154 __/__/__

Mini-challenge

✓

Compliment Marathon: Exchange 3 genuine compliments about each other in a row—no repeats allowed!

"We find rest in those we trust, and we provide a resting place in ourselves for those who trust us.", Thomas Moore

Day 155 __/__/__

Intimacy & vulnerability

♡

Shared Vulnerability: Do you believe vulnerability should always be mutual, or is it okay if one partner is more open than the other at times?

"To be close is to risk tears, but it also welcomes joy beyond measure.", Kahlil Gibran (adapted)

Day 156 __/__/__

Funny fun facts

Decor Disasters: What's the biggest decorating disaster you've had in your home? Did you fix it or live with it?

"If you want to sacrifice the admiration of many men for the criticism of one, go ahead —get married.", Katharine Hepburn (humorous line)

Day 157 __/__/__

Learn more about your partner

> **First Memory:** What's the first memory that comes to mind from your childhood? Why do you think it stands out?

"We deepen connection when we explore each other's inner worlds.", Harriet Lerner (idea paraphrased)

Day 158 __/__/__

Dreams and fantasies

Celebrity Life: If you could live the life of any celebrity for a day, who would you choose and what would you do?

"Dreams seen in tandem carry double the hope.", Henry David Thoreau (inspired)

Day 159 ___/___/___

Intimacy & vulnerability

♡

Emotional Burdens: How comfortable are you allowing someone to take care of you when you're feeling low or overwhelmed?

"Two hearts share one breath when they dare to reveal themselves.", Rumi (poetic paraphrase)

Day 160 __/__/____

Daring

Outdoor Shout: Open a window and shout something silly or romantic that your partner chooses.

"Two who dare to be real with each other become unstoppable.", Marianne Williamson (concept paraphrased)

Day 161 __/__/__

Weekly reflection

Shared Laugh: What's the funniest or most lighthearted moment you shared with your partner recently?

"In every glance exchanged, we either deepen the bond or let it slip away.", E.M. Forster
(idea paraphrased)

Day 162 __/__/__

Childhood & memories

Favorite School Subject: What was your favorite subject in school, and did it influence your life path later on?

"Telling someone about your childhood is like giving them your old map of the world.",
George Saunders (idea paraphrased)

Day 163 ___/___/___

Psychology

Overcoming Obstacles: Describe a time when you overcame a significant challenge. What did you learn about yourself through this experience?[1]

---

[1] The nature of the challenge and the approach to overcoming it can demonstrate your partner's resilience, problem-solving skills, and support needs.

Day 164 __/__/____

Shared experiences

Mystery Solving: Play an online escape room or mystery game where you both have to solve puzzles and clues (e.g. "We were here together")

"Simplicity in shared moments can yield the richest ties.", Laura Ingalls Wilder (concept paraphrased)

Day 165 __/__/__

Intimacy & vulnerability

♡

Unspoken Desires: Is there a personal desire, fantasy, or dream (relationship-wise) that you've hesitated to voice? Why?

"It is in the act of revealing, not concealing, that trust grows.", M. Scott Peck (concept paraphrased)

Day 166 __/__/__

Funny fun facts

Sleep Talking Shenanigans: Do you talk in your sleep? Share the funniest thing you've said, according to others.

"When a man opens a car door for his wife, it's either a new car or a new wife.",
Prince Philip

Day 167 __/__/__

Learn more about your partner

Travel Dream: Where is one place you've never been but feel drawn to? What attracts you to it?

"The closer you look, the more wonders you find.", Henry James (shortened paraphrase)

Day 168 __/__/____

Mini-challenge

✓

> **Guess My Day:** Challenge each other to guess specific details about each other's day (e.g., what did you eat for lunch?). See who's most accurate.

"A heart to serve and a mind to understand are the best companions in any relationship.", Unknown

Day 169 ___/___/___

Dreams and fantasies

> **Dream Collaboration:** Which artist, scientist, or leader, past or present, would you want to collaborate with on a project?

"Partners who daydream together chart a future unbounded by the present.", Marianne Williamson (concept paraphrased)

Day 170 __/__/__

Intimacy & vulnerability

♡

Willingness to Ask for Help: Do you find it hard to ask your partner for help, even in small things? What do you think causes that hesitation?

"It is in the act of revealing, not concealing, that trust grows.", M. Scott Peck (concept paraphrased)

Day 171 __/__/__

Daring

> **Silly Serenade:** Call and serenade a (mutual) friend with a funny song, on speakerphone so your partner can listen.

"Risk is the father of reward in any relationship worth having.", Paulo Freire (inspired paraphrase)

Day 172 __/__/____

Psychology

Values and Beliefs: List the top three values or beliefs you live by. Discuss how these guide your actions and decisions.[1]

---

[1] Core values guide behavior and decisions. Look for alignment or differences in your values to understand potential sources of harmony and conflict.

Day 173 __/__/__

Childhood & memories

Favorite Vacation: What's the most memorable family vacation or trip you took, and why does it stand out?

"Revisiting our roots together can heal fractures we didn't know we had.", Henry Cloud (concept paraphrased)

Day 174 __/__/__

Shared experiences

Wine or Beer Tasting: Have a virtual tasting session. Choose a selection of wines or beers available to both of you, and taste and discuss them over video.

"A shared sunset binds souls more deeply than a hundred dinners apart.", Antoine de Saint-Exupery (concept paraphrased, distinct from the listed quote)

Day 175 __/__/__

Weekly reflection

Affection Meter: How did you express love or appreciation to your partner this week, and vice versa?

"True tenderness is silent; only the deeper currents of the heart can speak it.", Ivan Turgenev (paraphrased)

Day 176 __/__/____

Intimacy & vulnerability

♡

Previous Heartbreak: How have past heartbreaks or disappointments affected your ability to be vulnerable now?

"The willingness to be open invites tenderness to bloom.", Osho (idea paraphrased)

Day 177 __/__/__

Fun & romance

Best Romantic Advice: What's the best piece of romantic or fun relationship advice you've ever received (or given)?

"True romance is in the simplest gestures done with genuine affection.", Nicholas Sparks (concept paraphrased)

Day 178 __/__/____

Shared future & goals

Impact on the World: Do you see us contributing to a cause or community project in the future? Which issues are we both passionate about?

"When your dreams align, each step forward feels like you're walking on air.", Nicholas Sparks (idea paraphrased)

Day 179 __/__/__

Learn more about your partner

Craftsmanship Appreciation: Is there a form of craftsmanship (like woodworking, knitting, etc.) you particularly admire? Why?

"Knowing someone is an endless journey if you dare to keep walking.", Toni Morrison (inspired paraphrase)

Day 180 __/__/__

Shared experiences

> **Cultural Exchange Night:** Each of you shares something special from your culture or hometown. It could be stories, local music, traditional dances, or even a cooking lesson.

"We strengthen each other when we stand as witnesses to one another's lives.", Rachel Naomi Remen (inspired)

Day 181 __/__/__

Daring

⚡

> **Improv Storytelling:** Start a live video and tell an improvised story based on words your partner gives you.

"When you leap together, even uncertainty feels like an adventure.", Unknown

Day 182 __/__/__

Mini-challenge

✓

Movie Night Sync: Choose the same movie or show to watch separately at the same time, then discuss live or afterward (Several Chrome extensions enable synced Netflix or YouTube viewing with chat).

"A sympathetic friend can be as dear as a brother.", Homer

Day 183 __/__/__

Communication & conflict

Emotional Triggers: Which topics (e.g., finances, family, past relationships) trigger your strongest reactions, and why?

"A discussion can turn destructive when respect leaves the room.", John Gottman (idea paraphrased, not in your restricted list)

Day 184 __/__/__

Learn more about your partner

Personal Evolution: How do you think you've changed most significantly over the past five years?

"Real closeness grows when you recognize how much you have yet to learn about each other.", Esther Perel (idea paraphrased)

Day 185 __/__/__

Daring

⚡

Wacky Hairstyle: Style your hair in the most outrageous way possible and wear it for the rest of the call.

"A ship may be safe in harbor, but that's not what ships are for—nor hearts.", John A. Shedd (common paraphrase; added 'hearts')

Day 186 __/__/__

Funny fun facts

Prank Gone Wrong: Have you ever attempted a prank that backfired spectacularly? What was the aftermath?

"My wife and I were happy for twenty years—then we met.", Rodney Dangerfield

Day 187 ___/___/___

Dreams and fantasies

Ultimate Road Trip: Describe your ultimate road trip adventure. Where would you go, and what would you do?

"Fantasies are the private wings on which relationships can soar.", Mark Twain (concept attributed, paraphrased)

Day 188 __/__/____

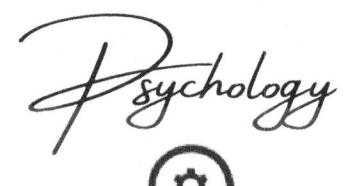

Psychology

The Comfort Zone Challenge: What's one thing outside your comfort zone you'd like to try? Discuss the importance of growth and trying new things.[1]

---

[1] The chosen activity can reveal your partner's aspirations and fears, as well as areas where they seek growth or change.

Day 189 ___/___/___

Weekly reflection

Self-Reflection Quote: If you had to choose a quote or mantra that captures this week, what would it be?

"Mutual joy is the sign of a partnership that sparks light in the darkness.", Edith Wharton (adapted)

Day 190 __/__/____

Intimacy & vulnerability

♡

> **Balancing Independence:** How do you balance being vulnerable with maintaining your own sense of independence?

. . . .
. . . .
. . . .
. . . .
. . . .
. . . .
. . . .
. . . .
. . . .
. . . .
. . . .
. . . .
. . . .
. . . .
. . . .
. . . .

"One does not truly see another until the masks come off.", C.S. Lewis (concept paraphrased, not the same as your restricted quote)

Day 191 __/__/__

Funny fun facts

Caught Dancing: Ever been caught dancing or singing when you thought you were alone? Who caught you?

"The secret of a happy marriage remains a secret.", Henny Youngman

Day 192 __/__/__

Daring

Public Compliment: Compliment the first person you see outside on something specific.

"We're more alive when we dare to face fear side by side.", Susan Jeffers (inspired)

Day 193 ___/___/___

Funny fun facts

Awkward Encounters: What's your most cringe-worthy encounter with someone you admired or found attractive?

"When you see a married couple walking down the street, the one that's a few steps ahead is the one that's mad.", Helen Rowland

Day 194 __/__/____

Dreams and fantasies

Fantasy Home: If you could design your fantasy home, what unique features would it include?

"When you share your wildest imaginings, you invite real closeness.", Joseph Campbell (inspired paraphrase)

Day 195 __/__/__

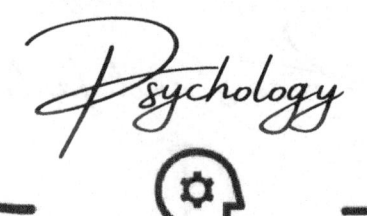

Psychology

Personality Traits: Identify one personality trait you admire in your partner and one you'd like to improve in yourself. Share and discuss how these traits affect your relationship.[1]

---

[1] Admired traits in you reflect what your partner values or desires in themselves. Traits they wish to improve upon reveal their self-awareness and personal development goals.

Day 196 __/__/____

Mini-challenge

✓

Bedtime Story: Call or record a short bedtime story or anecdote for your partner to listen to before sleeping.

"Kind words are more healing to a weary heart than any balm.", Sarah Fielding (18th-century writer)

Day 197 ___/___/___

Communication & conflict

Making Amends: What does a genuine apology look like to you, and how quickly do you typically offer or expect it?

"The road to resolution is paved with empathy and a willingness to hear what hurts.",
Sharon Salzberg (concept paraphrased)

Day 198 __/__/__

Childhood & memories

Impactful Teacher: Was there a teacher or mentor who left a lasting impression on you? How did they influence you?

"To see someone's childhood photos is to glimpse their original wonder.", Unknown

Day 199 __/__/__

Shared experiences

Book Club for Two: Choose a book to read simultaneously, then have weekly discussions about the chapters you've read.

"Two people fully present can transform an ordinary moment into something sacred.",
Pema Chodron (concept paraphrased)

Day 200 __/__/__

Funny fun facts

Misguided Makeover: Tried to give yourself a haircut or beauty treatment and it went horribly wrong? What was the damage?

"A perfect partner is someone who doesn't try to fix all your quirks—because they enjoy them too.", Unknown (often misattributed, but quoted humorously)

Day 201 __/__/__

Fun & romance

Shared Hobby: If we could learn a new hobby as a couple (cooking class, dancing, etc.), what would you want to try first?

"Playfulness keeps the heart youthful and the bond fresh.", Dr. Gary Chapman (idea paraphrased)

Day 202 __/__/____

Personal growth & aspirations

Celebrating Victories: How do you celebrate your successes or milestones, big or small?

"The highest aspiration is that we both become our best selves, together.", Maria Popova (idea paraphrased)

Day 203 __/__/__

Weekly reflection

Learning From Mistakes: Did you slip up somewhere? What did you learn from it?

"Cherish the one who hears your silence and answers without words.", D. H. Lawrence (inspired paraphrase)

Day 204 __/__/__

Communication & conflict

Balancing Calm & Honesty: Is it more important for you to remain calm or to express your raw emotions during a dispute?

"You learn the most about someone when they disagree with you.", Peter Thiel (business thinker, paraphrased)

Day 205 __/__/__

Dreams and fantasies

Time-Freezing Moment: If you could freeze time at any one moment, which moment would you choose and why?

"Break your routines; that's where joint discovery lies.", Anthony Robbins (paraphrased)

Day 206 __/__/__

Learn more about your partner

Moment of Laughter: Share a memory when you laughed uncontrollably. What was so funny?

"Ask and keep asking—the soul unfolds itself in layers.", Adrienne Rich (inspired paraphrase)

Day 207 __/__/__

Personal growth & aspirations

One Year From Now: Where do you see yourself (physically, emotionally, or professionally) one year from today?

"We do not learn from experience alone; we learn by reflecting on shared experiences.",
John Dewey (adapted)

Day 208 __/__/____

Childhood & memories

Weekend Ritual: What did a typical weekend look like for you as a child, and which part did you love the most?

"Memories hold the threads of who we are; weaving them together fosters unity.", Toni Morrison (inspired paraphrase)

Day 209 __/__/__

Shared experiences

Silly Debate Club: Have light-hearted debates on absurd topics, like "Is cereal soup?" or "Would you rather fight one horse-sized duck or a hundred duck-sized horses?"

"Joint experiences are the diaries of a couple's unfolding story.", Esther Perel (idea paraphrased)

Day 210 __/__/__

Mini-challenge

✓

Song Dedication: Each dedicate a song to the other that captures how you feel right now. Share the link or sing a snippet.

"In giving of yourself, you receive more than you ever had.", Antoine de Saint-Exupery (distinct from earlier quotes)

Day 211 __/__/__

Funny fun facts

😄

Costume Capers: What's the most ridiculous costume you've ever worn? Was it a hit or a miss?

"Relationships are like a walk in the park: Jurassic Park.", Unknown (popular humorous saying)

Day 212 __/__/____

Shared future & goals

Risk-Taking Future: Are you open to big life changes (career shifts, relocations) if the opportunity arises, or do you prefer stability?

"Only by holding hands toward tomorrow do we truly share today.", Henri J.M. Nouwen (inspired)

Day 213 __/__/__

Fun & romance

Surprise Random Acts: What random act of romance (love note, flowers, etc.) would you love to receive unexpectedly?

"There is no charm equal to the tenderness of a devoted heart.", Jane Austen (slightly adapted)

Day 214 __/__/__

Personal growth & aspirations

Pivot Points: Think of a major turning point in your life. How did it shape your aspirations?

"True partnership is helping each other reach a potential neither could achieve alone.",
Ambrose Redmoon (concept paraphrased)

Day 215 ___/___/___

Intimacy & vulnerability

♡

Fear of Judgment: Does the possibility of being judged ever keep you from sharing parts of yourself?

"Vulnerability breathes life into stagnant bonds.", bell hooks (concept paraphrased)

Day 216 __/__/____

Shared future & goals

Adventure Factor: Would you like to travel extensively together, maybe even live abroad, or do you prefer occasional vacations?

"To see a future in someone's eyes is to grant the present new meaning.", Emily Bronte (adapted concept)

Day 217 ___/___/___

Mini-challenge

✓

Good News Hunt: Both find one piece of positive news (local or global) to share and celebrate.

"Faith is the bird that feels the light and sings while the dawn is still dark.",
Rabindranath Tagore

Day 218 __/__/__

Shared experiences

Documentary Night: Watch a documentary together on a subject you're both interested in, followed by a discussion.

"In shared laughter, we find glimpses of a common soul.", Leo Rosten

Day 219 ___/___/___

Psychology

Emotional Intelligence: Share a situation where you had to exercise emotional intelligence. Discuss how being in tune with your emotions and those of others plays a role in your relationship.[1]

---

[1] Discussing emotional intelligence showcases your partner's ability to navigate emotional landscapes, emphasizing empathy, self-regulation, and social skills.

Day 220 __/__/____

Communication & conflict

Handling Criticism: How do you usually react to criticism, even if it's meant to be constructive?

"Speak your truth quietly and clearly; keep calm to truly connect.", Max Ehrmann (idea paraphrased from Desiderata)

Day 221 __/__/__

Childhood & memories

Neighborhood Hangout: Was there a special spot in your neighborhood where you and your friends always gathered?

"Speak fondly of your past, and you offer your partner a gentle corner of your heart.",
Jacqueline Woodson (concept paraphrased)

Day 222 __/__/____

Shared experiences

Tea Tasting: Order the same set of teas and have a tasting session to discuss your favorites and learn more about tea.

"No two souls reveal themselves at once; discovery requires patience.", Anais Nin (idea paraphrased, different from the listed quote)

Day 223 ___/___/___

Personal growth & aspirations

Inspiration Sources: Who or what inspires you the most when you feel stuck or unmotivated?

"When you invest in another's growth, you multiply your own.", Zig Ziglar (inspired)

Day 224 __/__/____

Weekly reflection

Emotional Bucket: Do you feel emotionally "full" or "depleted" at the end of this week? Why?

"A single day spent in unity can outweigh years of superficial coexistence.", Ralph Waldo Emerson (concept paraphrased)

Day 225 __/__/__

Psychology

The Role Model: Talk about someone you look up to and why. Discuss the qualities that make them a role model for you.[1]

---

[1] The qualities admired in a role model can hint at your partner's aspirations or the characteristics they strive to embody.

Day 226 __/__/__

Childhood & memories

Family Conflicts: Can you recall a childhood disagreement or conflict in the family and how it was resolved?

"When you share the laughter of your childhood, you let someone hear your original voice.", Mitch Albom (idea paraphrased)

Day 227 __/__/____

Funny fun facts

Text Troubles: Ever sent a text about someone to that very person by mistake? How did you recover?

"Love at first sight is easy to understand; it's when two people have been looking at each other for years that it becomes a miracle.", Sam Levenson (attributed)

Day 228 __/__/__

Intimacy & vulnerability

♡

Defusing Shame: Is there anything you've felt ashamed about in the past that you'd like to release or talk through with your partner?

"In unguarded moments, we glimpse the true beauty of each other.", Anais Nin

Day 229 ___/___/___

Communication & conflict

Boundaries in Arguments: Are there certain lines you believe should never be crossed during an argument, no matter what?

"A productive argument is one that leads both sides closer to the truth.", Karl Popper (concept paraphrased)

Day 230 __/__/__

Personal growth & aspirations

Balancing Strengths & Weaknesses: How do you acknowledge and work on your weaknesses without undermining your strengths?

"Support each other's becoming, and you create an unstoppable force.", Iyanla Vanzant (concept paraphrased)

Day 231 __/__/__

Mini-challenge

✓

Book Exchange: Recommend a book or article to read during the week. Next reflection day, share key takeaways.

"Let your heart hold fast to what it has once cherished.", Seneca (inspired paraphrase)

Day 232 ___/___/___

Shared future & goals

Conflict Resolution Roadmap: As we grow, how can we ensure we keep improving on how we handle disagreements?

"Partnership means forging a path, not just following one.", Simon Sinek (idea paraphrased)

Day 233 __/__/__

Fun & romance

Public Displays of Affection: How comfortable are you with PDAs, and is there a form of public affection you actually enjoy?

"Champagne is for celebrating together, even if it's just a Tuesday.", Donatella Versace (idea paraphrased)

Day 234 __/__/____

Shared experiences

Guided Meditation: Do a guided meditation session together to relax and connect on a deeper level.

"Collect memories, not things—especially with someone who wants to see the world through your eyes.", Alexandra Stoddard (concept paraphrased)

Day 235 __/__/__

Learn more about your partner

Act of Kindness: Describe a small act of kindness that made a big impact on you.

"Embrace the unknown in another's heart, and you'll never run out of questions.", Carl Jung (concept paraphrased)

Day 236 __/__/____

Dreams and fantasies

Mythical Encounter: If you could meet any mythical creature or character, who would it be and what would you ask them?

"Two hearts dreaming together form a single horizon.", Kahlil Gibran (distinct from quotes in your list, paraphrased)

Day 237 __/__/__

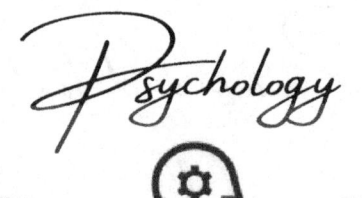

Psychology

Conflict Resolution: Describe your approach to resolving conflicts. Discuss how understanding each other's conflict resolution styles can strengthen your relationship.[1]

---

[1] Understanding each other's conflict resolution style can help navigate disagreements more effectively, emphasizing communication styles and needs during conflicts.

Day 238 __/__/____

Weekly reflection

New Perspective: Did anything happen that made you see an old situation in a new light?

"We truly meet each other in the space between our separate identities.", Martin Buber
(idea paraphrased)

Day 239 __/__/__

Funny fun facts

😄

Photo Fails: Got a hilariously bad photo of yourself? What's the story behind it?

"A guy knows he's in love when he loses interest in his car for a couple of days.", Tim Allen (comedian, paraphrased)

Day 240 __/__/____

Childhood & memories

Memorable Birthday: What was your most memorable birthday party or celebration, and what made it special?

"Under every adult longing is a child's unanswered question.", Carl Rogers (idea paraphrased)

Day 241 ___/___/___

Shared future & goals

Five-Year Timeline: Where would you like us to be (personally, professionally, emotionally) in five years, and what steps lead there?

"Couples united in purpose can move mountains.", Zig Ziglar (idea paraphrased)

Day 242 __/__/____

Intimacy & vulnerability

♡

Emotional Boundaries: Do you believe couples should have some emotional boundaries or secrets, or should everything be transparent?

"Closeness demands that we let someone see our faults and love us anyway.", Henri Nouwen (idea paraphrased)

Day 243 ___/___/___

Personal growth & aspirations

Preferred Environment: In what type of environment (physical or emotional) do you feel you thrive the most, and why?

"The glorious challenge of partnership is that it forces you to become who you're meant to be.", James Hollis (Jungian psychologist, paraphrased)

Day 244 __/__/____

Shared experiences

Bucket List Sharing: Share and discuss your personal bucket lists, finding common goals and dreaming together.

"True companionship is found in the footprints you leave together.", Unknown

Day 245 __/__/__

Mini-challenge

Goal Support: Each partner picks one small goal for the coming week (e.g., 2 extra glasses of water daily). Track and cheer each other on

"Life is partly what we make it, and partly what is made by the friends we choose.",
Tennessee Williams

Day 246 __/__/__

Learn more about your partner

Favored Childhood Activity: What was your favorite thing to do as a child during summer?

"When you believe there's more to learn, that's when true intimacy begins.", Erich Fromm (idea paraphrased)

Day 247 __/__/__

Fun & romance

Guilty Pleasure Dates: Is there a "cheesy" or cliché romantic activity (like a horse-drawn carriage ride) you secretly want to try?

"Dancing together, even if you can't dance, is romance in motion.", Hugh Jackman (inspired paraphrase)

Day 248 __/__/____

Funny fun facts

Dare to Despair: What's the funniest dare you've ever accepted? Did you regret it?

"All tragedies are finished by a death, all comedies by a marriage.", Lord Byron

Day 249 __/__/__

Shared future & goals

Shared Business or Projects: Would you ever consider starting a business or creative project together, and if so, in what field?

"Share your hopes boldly, for half-kept dreams grow feeble in the dark.", Les Brown (concept paraphrased)

Day 250 __/__/____

Personal growth & aspirations

> **Turning Negatives into Positives:** Can you share a setback that turned out to be a catalyst for a much-needed change in your life?

"Aspire not just to unite, but to evolve together.", Rollo May (idea paraphrased, different from the quotes you listed)

Day 251 ___/___/___

Learn more about your partner

Personal Milestone: What personal milestone are you most proud of achieving?

"Be eager to understand rather than to confirm what you already think.", Stephen R. Covey (adapted concept)

Day 252 __/__/__

Weekly reflection

Quality Time: Reflect on how much quality time you and your partner had. How can you improve it next week?

"Two hearts that fuse their hopes and fears become an unstoppable force.", Thomas Merton (concept paraphrased)

Day 253 __/__/__

Shared experiences

Astrology Night: Look up your horoscopes and discuss whether you find them accurate or amusing.

"Small adventures often forge the greatest bonds.", Amelia Earhart (inspired paraphrase)

Day 254 __/__/____

Funny fun facts

Party Perplexities: What's the strangest party you've ever attended? What made it unforgettable?

"Happiness in marriage is a matter of pure chance, or so my dear mother used to say.",
Jane Austen (in Pride and Prejudice, paraphrased)

Day 255 ___/___/___

Communication & conflict

Cultural Influences: Has your cultural background shaped how you communicate or deal with conflict? How so?

"Listen not only to words but to the feelings they carry.", Carl Rogers

Day 256 ___/___/___

Personal growth & aspirations

Support System: Who or what makes up your support system, and how do they contribute to your aspirations?

"In helping each other grow, we plant the seeds of our own blooming.", Thich Nhat Hanh (concept paraphrased, distinct from your restricted list)

Day 257 __/__/__

Childhood & memories

Earliest Gratitude: What's the earliest memory you have of feeling genuinely thankful for something?

"To be fully known includes the child you once were.", Fred Rogers (inspired)

Day 258 __/__/____

Learn more about your partner

Favorite Time of Day: Do you have a favorite time of day? What do you like to do during this time?

"Discovery of another person is the single greatest adventure the human heart can undertake.", Leo Tolstoy (inspired, paraphrased)

Day 259 __/__/__

Mini-challenge

✓

Dance Challenge: Send each other a 30-second clip of you dancing to a favorite song. No judgments—just fun!

"When we stop judging, we create space to truly connect.", Ram Dass (concept paraphrased)

Day 260 __/__/__

Shared experiences

Personal Quiz Night: Create personal quizzes for each other to see how well you know one another.

"Sharing your world is the prelude to sharing your heart.", Brene Brown (concept paraphrased, distinct from her listed quotes)

Day 261 ___/___/___

Psychology

Your Legacy: How do you want to be remembered by others? Discuss how your actions today are contributing to the legacy you wish to leave.[1]

---

[1] Discussing legacies can uncover your partner's long-term goals and how they wish to impact the world or be remembered by others.

Day 262 __/__/__

Daring

Childhood Photo Recreation: Find an old childhood photo of yourself (or from your family album) and try to recreate it now—pose, outfit, and expression. Snap a pic of the result.

"Fortune sides with him who dares.", Virgil

Day 263 __/__/__

Fun & romance

Favorite Compliment: What's the best, most memorable compliment you've ever received from me?

"Humor is a powerful aphrodisiac; it breaks tension and fosters closeness.", Helen Fisher (anthropologist, paraphrased)

Day 264 __/__/____

Communication & conflict

Conflict Avoidance: Do you have a tendency to avoid conflict altogether? What are the pros and cons of that approach?

"Small misunderstandings can grow large if left unspoken; talk them out early.",
Unknown

Day 265 __/__/__

Dreams and fantasies

Space Exploration: If you could visit any planet or moon, where would you go and what would you hope to discover?

"If you can dream it alone, dream it better together.", Walt Disney (idea paraphrased)

Day 266 __/__/____

Weekly reflection

Energy Source: What activity or thought recharged your energy the most this week?

"You can measure the strength of a bond by how gently the two handle each other's weaknesses.", Auguste Rodin (inspired paraphrase)

Day 267 __/__/__

Personal growth & aspirations

What Does Fulfillment Look Like?: If you woke up tomorrow living your most fulfilled life, what would be different from today?

"Aligned goals in a relationship turn aspirations into achievements.", John C. Maxwell
(concept paraphrased)

Day 268 __/__/____

Childhood & memories

> **First Disappointment:** What was your first significant disappointment as a kid, and how did you cope with it?

"Sometimes the best way to move forward as a couple is to look back, hand in hand.",
Unknown

Day 269 ___/___/___

Learn more about your partner

Unusual Skill: Do you have an unusual skill or party trick? How did you learn it?

"You never really finish discovering someone who holds a piece of your heart.", Janet Fitch (idea paraphrased)

Day 270 __/__/____

Shared future & goals

Health & Wellness: How do you picture our shared approach to staying healthy—physically, mentally, spiritually—over time?

"Two souls with one horizon see possibilities multiplied, not just doubled.", Pierre Teilhard de Chardin (inspired)

Day 271 __/__/__

Communication & conflict

Active Listening Cues: Which body language or verbal cues help you feel that your partner is truly listening?

"True dialogue is when each person risks being changed by what the other says.", David Bohm (concept paraphrased)

Day 272 __/__/__

Funny fun facts

Elevator Escapades: Any funny or awkward elevator moments to share?

"My wife and I have the secret to a good marriage: twice a week, we go to a nice restaurant. She goes Tuesdays, I go Fridays.", Henny Youngman

Day 273 __/__/__

Mini-challenge

✓

Compliment Chain: For 24 hours, respond to any negative comment your partner makes (about themselves or the world) with a genuine compliment or positive twist.

"Let yourself be silently drawn by the stronger pull of what you truly desire.", Rumi

Day 274 __/__/__

Dreams and fantasies

Dream City: If you could design your dream city, what unique features would it have and why?

"The best relationships are those that allow space for the impossible to become real.",
bell hooks (concept paraphrased)

Day 275 __/__/____

Childhood & memories

Immersive Imagination: What sorts of imaginative games or "pretend play" did you enjoy the most?

"The child within you recognizes the child within me, and thus we understand each other's scars.", C.G. Jung (concept paraphrased)

Day 276 __/__/____

Shared experiences

Write a Story Together: Take turns writing sentences or paragraphs to create a story together, letting your imaginations run wild.

"We remember moments, not days, and those shared moments become our tapestry.",
Cesare Pavese (inspired paraphrase)

Day 277 __/__/__

Fun & romance

> **Serenade Me:** Would you ever sing to me (even if off-key), or is there another way you'd prefer to show your romantic side?

"Put a little mischief in your shared life, and watch the spark ignite.", Roald Dahl (concept paraphrased)

Day 278 __/__/____

Personal growth & aspirations

> **Influential Book:** Is there a book (or movie/podcast) that significantly shifted your perspective or goals?

"Two people truly connected accelerate each other's progress in life.", Brian Tracy (idea paraphrased)

Day 279 __/__/__

Intimacy & vulnerability

♡

Nonverbal Cues: What nonverbal signs from your partner instantly make you feel more at ease or more exposed?

"When you share your deepest fears, you free each other.", Thich Nhat Hanh (concept paraphrased, not in your restricted list)

Day 280 __/__/____

Weekly reflection

Letting Go: Is there a worry or tension you finally let go of? How did it feel?

"In partnership, the question shifts from 'What do I want?' to 'What do we need?'",
Margaret Mead (concept paraphrased)

Day 281 ___/___/___

Childhood & memories

First Crush: Who was your first childhood crush, and what do you remember about how you felt?

"We could never have cherished the earth so well if we had no childhood in it.", George Eliot (adapted from The Mill on the Floss)

Day 282 __/__/____

Communication & conflict

Agree to Disagree: In what situations do you think it's best to "agree to disagree," and how do you move on peacefully?

"We are not on opposite sides; we are on the same side against the problem.", Steve Goodier (idea paraphrased)

Day 283 __/__/__

Shared future & goals

Defining "Success" Together: What does success as a couple look like to you—financial security, happiness, legacy, etc.?

"A shared plan is the blueprint for building the home of your love.", Gary Chapman (concept paraphrased)

Day 284 ___/___/___

Shared experiences

Origami Challenge: Choose origami figures to try and fold together, comparing your final creations.

"The best souvenirs from life's journeys are the stories we gather together.", Unknown

Day 285 __/__/__

Funny fun facts

😄

Public Transport Tangle: Have you ever taken the wrong bus or train and found yourself in a funny or awkward adventure?

"By all means marry; if you get a good wife, you'll become happy; if you get a bad one, you'll become a philosopher.", Socrates

Day 286 __/__/__

Daring

30-Second Infomercial: Grab any random household item and deliver a passionate 30-second "infomercial" sales pitch about why everyone needs it.

"Everything you've ever wanted is on the other side of fear.", George Addair

Day 287 __/__/__

Mini-challenge

Themed Video Call: Choose a silly or fun theme (e.g., hats, PJs) and both dress accordingly for your next call.

"Friendship multiplies the good of life and divides its troubles.", Baltasar Gracian

Day 288 __/__/__

Childhood & memories

Influential Cartoon or TV Show: Which cartoon or TV show captured your imagination the most, and why?

"All of us are products of our childhood.", Michael Jackson

Day 289 __/__/__

Intimacy & vulnerability

♡

Common Vulnerabilities: What vulnerability do you think you and your partner share, and how can that be a point of connection?

"To accept another soul at their most fragile is the essence of profound intimacy.", John O'Donohue (idea paraphrased)

Day 290 __/__/__

Communication & conflict

Yelling vs. Whispering: Have you ever tried lowering your voice in an argument instead of raising it? What was the effect?

"The biggest communication problem is that we do not listen to understand; we listen to reply.", Stephen R. Covey (paraphrased)

Day 291 __/__/__

Shared future & goals

Social Circle: Do you see us cultivating a close-knit community of friends, or keeping a smaller circle as we move forward?

"One of the greatest gifts you can give each other is a united tomorrow.", Jim Rohn
(idea paraphrased)

Day 292 __/__/__

Personal growth & aspirations

Passion vs. Necessity: How do you balance pursuing what you love with meeting life's practical needs?

"The more you nurture your partner's dreams, the more you see them shine—and reflect light on you.", Marianne Williamson (idea paraphrased)

Day 293 ___/___/___

Daring

⚡

Out-of-Context Compliments: Send three short, genuine compliments in a row to a friend or coworker (anyone but your partner), totally out of the blue. Screenshot their response to share.

"Only those who dare to fail greatly can ever achieve greatly.", Robert F. Kennedy

Day 294 __/__/____

Weekly reflection

Curiosity Spark: Did you get curious about a topic or skill you'd like to explore more?

"To feel complete with another is to uncover pieces of yourself you never knew were missing", Sarah Ban Breathnach (inspired)

Day 295 __/__/__

Shared experiences

Scavenger Hunt: Create a list of items to find in your respective homes and race to see who can find them all first.

"In partnership, each experience is magnified by the hearts that live it.", Unknown

Day 296 ___/___/___

Communication & conflict

Conflict Aftermath: How do you typically feel right after a big argument—relieved, guilty, drained, or something else?

"Conflict is inevitable; if handled well, it can lead to deeper closeness.", Harriet Lerner (concept paraphrased)

Day 297 __/__/____

Funny fun facts

Slippery Slope: What's your most cartoonish slip or trip in public? Did anyone come to your rescue, or just watch it happen?

"Marriage is like twirling a baton or eating with chopsticks: It looks easy until you try it.", Helen Rowland

Day 298 __/__/__

Fun & romance

Perfect Evening In: If we're staying in for a romantic evening, what does your ideal setup look like—food, ambiance, activities?

"Romance thrives on creativity: a love note, a silly surprise, a whispered wish.", Gabrielle Zevin (paraphrased)

Day 299 ___/___/___

Childhood & memories

Childhood Injuries: Did you ever get hurt doing something mischievous or adventurous as a kid? Share the story.

"Childhood is the one story that stands by itself in every soul.", Ivan Doig

Day 300 __/__/__

Learn more about your partner

Life's Simple Pleasures: What small, everyday thing brings you joy?

"True connection grows as we unravel the stories that made each other who we are.",
Rachel Naomi Remen (idea paraphrased)

Day 301 __/__/__

Mini-challenge

Ugly Selfie Duel: Each person snaps the most ridiculous selfie they can and sends it to the other. Vote on who pulled off the funniest face!

"We come to each other in fragments, yet wholeness is found in our shared embrace.",
Edna St. Vincent Millay (poetic paraphrase)

Day 302 __/__/__

Dreams and fantasies

Dream Retreat: Describe your ideal retreat. Where is it located, and what activities do you envision there?

"The best relationships are those that allow space for the impossible to become real.",
bell hooks (concept paraphrased)

Day 303 ___/___/___

Communication & conflict

Conflict Patterns: Do you see any recurring pattern or cycle in your arguments, and how might you break it?

"Between what is said and not meant, and what is meant and not said, most understanding is lost.", Kahlil Gibran (adapted)

Day 304 ___/___/___

Funny fun facts

Time Warp Confusion: Ever shown up for an event or appointment on the completely wrong day and had to figure out a graceful exit?

"Never laugh at your spouse's choices—you are one of them.", Unknown

Day 305 __/__/__

Shared experiences

Photo Editing Fun: Edit photos of each other or of shared memories in humorous or artistic ways, then share and discuss your creations.

"Memories become lifelines, holding two souls across time and distance.", Patti Callahan Henry (concept paraphrased)

Day 306 __/__/____

Learn more about your partner

Historical Era: If you could experience life in another historical era, which one would it be and why?

"The best journeys happen when you never stop exploring who stands beside you.",
Morgan Harper Nichols (paraphrased)

Day 307 __/__/__

Shared future & goals

Crisis Plan: How do you imagine us handling big life crises (job loss, health issues) to come out stronger as a team?

"Committing to a future with another is an act of radical hope.", Rebecca Solnit
(concept paraphrased)

Day 308 __/__/__

Mini-challenge

✓

Sing-It-Don't-Say-It: For one day (or one conversation), you have to respond by singing your replies in any style—opera, country, rap. Guaranteed giggles.

"There is only one happiness in this life: to cherish and be cherished.", George Sand (adapted)

Day 309 __/__/__

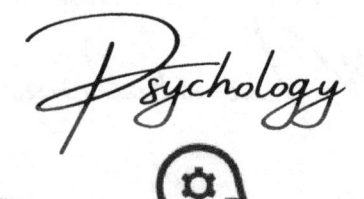

Psychology

The Unsent Letter: Write a letter to someone you've never properly thanked or apologized to. Discuss the feelings this brings up and the importance of closure.[1]

---

[1] Reveals unresolved emotions, the importance of certain relationships, and the need for closure or expression of gratitude or apology.

Day 310 __/__/__

Dreams and fantasies

Secret Society: If you could start a secret society, what would its purpose be and who would you invite to join?

"When your fantasies align, you find the portal to deeper intimacy.", Rumi (poetic adaptation)

Day 311 ___/___/___

Communication & conflict

Balancing Emotions: What's a strategy you use to stay emotionally balanced when you start feeling overwhelmed in a disagreement?

"We have two ears and one mouth so that we can listen twice as much as we speak.",
Epictetus

Day 312 __/__/____

Intimacy & vulnerability

♡

Reassuring Your Partner: When your partner expresses vulnerability, how do you typically respond, and is there a better way to show support?

"If you open your heart, you might get hurt, but if you don't, you'll never truly live.",
Louise Hay

Day 313 __/__/__

Shared future & goals

Future Hobbies: Is there a hobby or pastime you envision us enjoying together when we have more free time later in life?

"Sow your aspirations together, and watch the harvest sustain you both.", Joel Osteen (paraphrased concept)

Day 314 __/__/____

Shared experiences

Podcast Listening Party: Select a podcast episode to listen to together, then discuss your thoughts and takeaways.

"Two who share the same sense of wonder seldom lose their way.", Amelia Barr (adapted)

Day 315 __/__/__

Weekly reflection

One Word Summary: If you had to describe your week in one word, what would it be? Explain briefly.

"Two souls connected can cross any bridge, no matter how shaky.", Oprah Winfrey (idea paraphrased)

Day 316

Learn more about your partner

Bucket List Skill: Is there a skill not yet on your bucket list that you'd love to learn? What's stopping you?

"To discover another person is an art requiring humility and endless wonder.", Simone Weil (inspired paraphrase)

Day 317 __/__/__

Personal growth & aspirations

Resilience Strategies: When life throws you curveballs, what's your go-to method to bounce back?

"Our highest quest as partners is to lift one another toward the horizon of our gifts.",
Jean Vanier (concept paraphrased)

Day 318 ___/___/___

Intimacy & vulnerability

Creating Safe Conversations: What would make a conversation truly "safe" for both partners to share without holding back?

"Real closeness sees beyond the cracks and loves the light shining through them.",
Leonard Cohen (inspired by "cracks" concept)

Day 319 __/__/__

Funny fun facts

😄

Dream Delirium: Have you ever had such a bizarre dream that you woke up feeling confused about whether it was real or not? What happened in it?

"When in doubt, cuddle it out.", Unknown

Day 320 __/__/__

Dreams and fantasies

Wondrous Item: If you could possess any magical item from a book or movie, what would it be and how would you use it?

"A shared dream is a vow to meet each other in the realm of possibility.", Toni Morrison (inspired)

Day 321 __/__/__

Shared future & goals

Celebrating Milestones: What kinds of milestones (besides birthdays and anniversaries) do you hope we celebrate together?

"Where there is a shared tomorrow, there is strength in every today.", John Ortberg (idea paraphrased)

Day 322 __/__/____

Mini-challenge

✓

Goofy Fact Swap: Each of you digs up one random, bizarre fact (e.g., "Bananas are berries, but strawberries aren't!") and shares it. Discuss the weirdness or see if you can stump each other.

"Those who bring sunshine into the lives of others cannot keep it from themselves.", J.M. Barrie

Day 323 ___/___/___

Personal growth & aspirations

Using Past Mistakes: How do you use past mistakes or failures as building blocks for future success?

"However many holy words you read, what good will they do if you do not act on them?", Buddha

Day 324 __/__/____

Shared experiences

Karaoke Night: Use a karaoke app or YouTube karaoke videos to sing your favorite songs to each other.

"Shared adversity forges bonds that cannot be easily broken.", John Steinbeck (idea paraphrased)

Day 325 __/__/__

Daring

⚡

> **30-Second Meltdown:** Pretend you're an actor in an overly dramatic soap opera scene—go all out in a mock 'meltdown' for 30 seconds on camera.

"If you're not willing to risk the unusual, you will have to settle for the ordinary.", Jim Rohn

Day 326 __/__/___

Fun & romance

Mischevious Fun: If we could pull a harmless prank or playful challenge together, what would it be?

"A playful heart rarely loses the spark of enchantment.", Walt Whitman (inspired paraphrase)

Day 327 ___/___/___

Shared future & goals

Adoption of Pets: If we haven't already, how do you feel about having pets—dogs, cats, or something else—and what role do they play in our future?

"The future depends on what you do today.", Mahatma Gandhi

Day 328 __/__/____

Personal growth & aspirations

Goal Accountability: Do you prefer to keep your goals private or share them with others for accountability, and why?

"We are what we repeatedly do. Excellence, then, is not an act but a habit." Aristotle

Day 329 ___/___/___

Weekly reflection

Biggest Smile: Which moment (related to your partner or not) brought the biggest smile to your face?

"Forging a meaningful bond is the daily choice to understand rather than judge.", Tara Brach (concept paraphrased)

Day 330 __/__/__

Intimacy & vulnerability

♡

Receiving Compliments: How do you typically react to compliments or praise, and what does that say about your comfort with being seen?

"Comfort in exposing your wounds is the ultimate sign of trust.", Sarah Dessen (idea paraphrased)

Day 331 __/__/__

Communication & conflict

Verbal vs. Nonverbal: In conflict, do you pick up more on what's said or how it's said (tone, facial expressions, posture)?

"Peace is not the absence of conflict, but the ability to handle conflict by peaceful means.", Ronald Reagan

Day 332 __/__/____

Childhood & memories

Best or Worst Gift: What's the best or worst gift you ever received as a child, and how did you react?

"The childhood shows the man, as morning shows the day.", John Milton

Day 333 ___/___/___

Learn more about your partner

Wish for the World: If you could wish for one change in the world, what would it be and why?

"A gentle question can reveal more of a companion's truth than a thousand assumptions.", John M. Gottman (distinct paraphrase)

Day 334 __/__/____

Shared future & goals

Retirement Locale: Where do you picture living in your later years—a sunny beach, a cabin in the woods, near grandchildren, etc.?

"Alone we can do so little; together we can do so much.", Helen Keller

Day 335 __/__/__

Shared experiences

Wish Jar Creation: Each write down wishes or goals for your relationship and share them, discussing how you can achieve them together.

"When the journey is walked by two, every milestone echoes more deeply.", Bryant McGill (concept paraphrased)

Day 336 __/__/____

Mini-challenge

Whisper Challenge (Video Version): One partner wears headphones blasting music while the other mouths a silly phrase. The headphone-wearer tries to guess what was said. Hilarity guaranteed.

"To be fully seen by somebody, and be loved anyhow, is a miraculous gift.", Elizabeth Gilbert

Day 337 __/__/__

Psychology

The Alternate Path: If you had chosen a different career or path in life, what would it have been? Explore the reasons for this alternate choice and what it reveals about your interests.[1]

---

[1] Highlights hidden passions, unexplored talents, or regrets, offering insight into your partner's diverse interests and potential life courses.

Day 338 __/__/____

Personal growth & aspirations

> **Persistence vs. Letting Go:** Is there a goal you once chased but later decided to abandon? What did you learn from that?

"If you can't fly, then run. If you can't run, then walk. But by all means, keep moving."
— Martin Luther King Jr.

Day 339 __/__/__

Dreams and fantasies

Alien Encounter: If you could meet an alien, what would you ask them and what would you show them about Earth?

"Sometimes the bravest step is letting someone see the future you secretly crave.",
Brene Brown (inspired paraphrase)

Day 340 __/__/____

Shared future & goals

Career vs. Family Priorities: If we needed to choose between career moves or family needs, how would we negotiate that together?

"If you want to lift yourself up, lift up someone else.", Booker T. Washington

Day 341 __/__/__

Childhood & memories

If You Could Relive One Day: Which single day from your childhood would you choose to relive, and why?

"Memories of childhood were dreams that lingered after waking.", Julian Barnes

Day 342 __/__/__

Funny fun facts

😄

Language Blunder: Have you ever tried speaking a new language and ended up saying something completely mortifying by accident?

"Most couples have two minds, but only one TV remote.", Unknown

Day 343 ___/___/___

Weekly reflection

Mindset Shift: Is there a mindset or belief you decided to challenge this week?

"In the sanctuary of togetherness, we become guardians of each other's dreams.", Jean Vanier (idea paraphrased)

Day 344 __/__/__

Intimacy & vulnerability

♡

Revealing Weaknesses: What "weakness" are you learning to embrace as part of who you are?

"Don't smother each other. No one can grow in the shade.", Leo Buscaglia

Day 345 __/__/__

Shared future & goals

Annual Check-Ins: Would you be open to having an annual "relationship check-in" to set goals and reflect on progress?

"Purpose shared is purpose strengthened.", Charles Eisenstein (inspired paraphrase)

Day 346 __/__/____

Personal growth & aspirations

Seeking Guidance: Do you find it easier to seek guidance from people you know, or do you prefer to figure things out independently?

"What lies behind us and what lies before us are small matters compared to what lies within us.", Henry Stanley Haskins (often misattributed)

Day 347 ___/___/___

Dreams and fantasies

> **Time Capsule Message:** If you could send a message to the future in a time capsule, what would you say and to whom?

"Where hearts agree, fantasies evolve into realities.", Paulo Coelho (adapted concept)

Day 348 ___/___/___

Funny fun facts

Social Media Slip-ups: Ever posted something on social media that you immediately regretted? What was it?

"If you want your partner's full attention, talk in your sleep.", Unknown

Day 349 __/__/__

Psychology

The Solitude Moment: What do you most enjoy doing when you're alone? This can highlight personal needs for space, creativity, or relaxation.[1]

---

[1] Shows what activities or practices your partner values for personal fulfillment, relaxation, or self-reflection.

Day 350 __/__/____

Mini-challenge

✓

One-Color Meal: Challenge each other to prepare or plate a meal (or snack) that's predominantly one color—bonus points for humor in presentation. Share the culinary "masterpiece" photos.

"We live by admiration, hope, and care; as these are well-rooted, we flourish.", William Wordsworth (slightly adapted)

Day 351 __/__/__

Daring

Dare: Humorously roast yourself for 30 seconds straight—point out all your own goofy quirks and silly habits. Record it without stopping or laughing

"You can never cross the ocean unless you have the courage to lose sight of the shore.",
Attributed to Christopher Columbus

Day 352 __/__/__

Fun & romance

> **Goofiness Meter:** Do you ever hold back your goofy side around me, or do you feel safe letting it out completely?

"Romance is the laughter that arises when souls meet on a joyful plane.", Victor Hugo (idea paraphrased)

Day 353 ___/___/___

Communication & conflict

Repair Attempts: Do you believe in making quick "repair attempts" (like humor or hugs) during a conflict, or should you wait until it's fully resolved?

"Communicate unto others what you would want them to communicate unto you.", Aaron Goldman (variation on the Golden Rule)

Day 354 ___/___/___

Dreams and fantasies

🌙

Underwater Adventure: If you could breathe underwater, where would you explore and what sea creatures would you hope to see?

"A dream you dream alone is only a dream. A dream you dream together is reality.",
John Lennon

Day 355 ___/___/___

Personal growth & aspirations

> **Measuring Growth:** How do you measure or recognize that you're growing—through external achievements, internal changes, or both?

"Our greatest glory is not in never falling, but in rising every time we fall.", Confucius

Day 356 ___/___/___

Childhood & memories

Lesson Learned: Share a time you got in trouble or made a mistake as a kid that ended up teaching you a valuable lesson.

"We often live our lives by the stories we tell about our past.", Barbara Kingsolver (concept paraphrased)

Day 357 __/__/__

Mini-challenge

✓

Out-of-Context Quotes: Throughout the day, each partner sends the other random out-of-context quotes from movies or books. The more random and outlandish, the funnier it gets when you try to decipher them.

"Love is a serious mental disease.", Plato

Day 358 __/__/____

Learn more about your partner

The Unsung Hobby: What hobby would you pursue if time and money were no object?

"Knowing another deeply is a dance of curiosity and patience, step by step.", Mark Nepo (concept paraphrased)

Day 359 __/__/____

Shared future & goals

End-of-Life Wishes: It can be tough to talk about, but do you have ideas about the kind of legacy or final arrangements you'd prefer, and how can we support each other's wishes?

"A shared vision is proof that two hearts believe in the same tomorrow.", Unknown

Day 360 __/__/____

Communication & conflict

Conflict Success Story: Can you recall a specific argument that actually brought you closer in the end? What made it different?

"He who knows does not speak; he who speaks does not know.", Lao Tzu

Day 361 __/__/__

Funny fun facts

Uncontrollable Giggles: Has something totally normal ever triggered a laughing fit you just couldn't stop, especially at the worst possible time?

"The four most important words in any marriage: 'I'll do the dishes.'", Unknown

Day 362 __/__/____

Dreams and fantasies

> **Historical Witness:** If you could witness any event in history firsthand, what would it be and why?

"Those who dream by day are aware of many things hidden from those who dream only by night.", Edgar Allan Poe

Day 363 ___/___/___

Childhood & memories

Favorite Childhood Recipe: Was there a special meal, dessert, or snack from your childhood that you still think about fondly?

"In every adult lurks a child—an eternal becoming.", C.G. Jung

Day 364 __/__/__

Weekly reflection

Partner Appreciation: What's one thing your partner did this week that you really appreciated but didn't fully express?

"Every time we truly connect, we rewrite our shared story to include a deeper truth.",
Donald Miller (concept paraphrased)

Day 365 ___/___/___

Yearly reflection

Congratulations on reaching this remarkable milestone! You've just completed a full year of self-discovery, heartfelt conversations, and meaningful moments shared. Reflect on how far you've come—every answer, every challenge, every bit of laughter and vulnerability has shaped you into who you are today. As you close this book, may the insights you've gained inspire you to continue exploring, growing, and nurturing the bonds that matter most. Here's to the journey behind you—and all the new adventures waiting ahead!

"Love is the absence of judgment.", Dalai Lama

What's next?

Congratulations on completing this year-long journey of daily reflections, questions, and shared moments! You've likely learned more about yourself, your partner, and the unique bond you both share. But growth doesn't stop here.

- **Continue the Conversation**: Keep having open, curious discussions beyond these pages. Ask follow-up questions and revisit old prompts if you want to see how your answers have evolved.
- **Celebrate Milestones**: Whether it's weekly check-ins or a monthly "date night" review, take time to appreciate how far you've come—together.
- **Try New Experiences**: Pick a few bucket-list activities or experiences you've talked about in this book and make concrete plans to fulfill them.
- **Keep the Spark Alive**: Small gestures matter. Keep writing each other notes, planning surprises, and never stop discovering new reasons to fall in love all over again.

Above all, remember that every day is a chance to grow closer. Here's to a future filled with understanding, laughter, and lasting connection!

Made in the USA
Las Vegas, NV
26 February 2025